ATOMS and MOLECULES

Investigating the Building Blocks of Matter

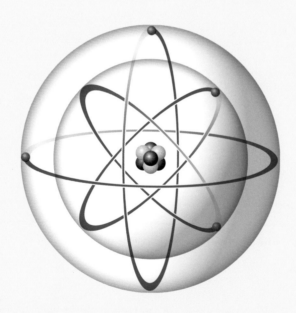

CHRIS WOODFORD AND MARTIN CLOWES

rosen publishing's
rosen
central®

New York

This edition first published in 2013 by:

The Rosen Publishing Group, Inc.
29 East 21st Street
New York, NY 10010

Consultant: Don Franceschetti, Ph.D., Distinguished Service Professor, Departments of Physics and Chemistry, The University of Memphis, Memphis, Tennessee

Creative Director: Jeni Child
Picture Researcher: Helen Simm
Illustrators: Darren Awuah,
 Richard Burgess, and Mark Walker
Managing Editor: Tim Harris
Children's Publisher: Anne O'Daly
Production Director: Alastair Gourlay
Editorial Director: Lindsey Lowe

Library of Congress Cataloging-in-Publication Data

Woodford, Chris.
Atoms and molecules: investigating the building blocks of matter/Chris Woodford, Martin Clowes.—1st ed.
  p. cm.—(Scientific pathways)
Includes bibliographical references and index.
ISBN 978-1-4488-7196-4 (library binding)
1. Atoms—Juvenile literature. 2. Molecules—Juvenile literature. 3. Matter—Juvenile literature. I. Clowes, Martin. II. Title.
QC173.16.W664 2013
539'.1—dc23

2011044498

Manufactured in the United States of America

CPSIA Compliance Information: Batch #S12YA: For further information, contact Rosen Publishing, New York, New York, at 1-800-237-9932.

CONTENTS

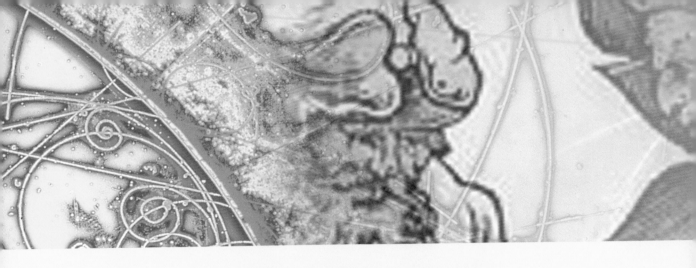

INTRODUCTION

Matter is the scientific name for the material that makes up everything around us—ourselves, the air we breathe, the ground on which we stand, and everything we can touch or smell. Matter is formed by atoms and molecules.

MATTER IS ALL AROUND US. IT is formed by individual atoms that are many thousands of times too small to see through a microscope. Atoms are such tiny structures that until the twentieth century, scientists had no firm proof that they even existed.

The notion that matter might consist of atoms occurred to a few Greek philosophers almost two thousand five hundred years ago. The idea did not catch on. Most Greek philosophers believed four or five basic substances combined to produce all matter. Their theory had no place for atoms.

The theory of atoms resurfaced in the late seventeenth century when chemists started to work in an organized way. They found several basic substances that they could not split into simpler substances. Chemists called these substances chemical elements.

Centuries passed before scientists formulated modern ideas about the atoms that formed the elements.

The idea that atoms join to make larger, more complicated structures called molecules first appeared in the nineteenth century. The theory of molecules not only helps us understand why many chemical substances behave as they do but also explains why solids, liquids, and gases behave differently from one another.

Modern theories about the structure of atoms emerged around the start of the twentieth century. Physicists then discovered the fragments that make up atoms: electrons, neutrons, and protons.

Experiments suggested that neutrons and protons clump together at the core of each atom in a tight bundle, called the nucleus. Scientists then set about determining how electrons fit in or around the nucleus.

Quantum theory explores the structure of individual atoms and explains how atoms group together to form molecules. The science of quantum mechanics has enabled chemists to predict and then discover new substances with unusual and useful properties. Physicists have been exploring electrons, neutrons, and protons to see if they consist of yet smaller bits of matter.

1 | THE EARLIEST THEORIES

The ancient Greek philosophers believed that matter consisted of mixtures of four or five basic elements (substances). Later, alchemists tried to turn common metals, such as lead, into precious gold.

ANCIENT GREEK PHILOSOPHERS developed theories of matter based on what they saw around them. In the ninth century BCE, Thales of Miletus noticed that all living things need water to survive. He suggested water was the basis of all matter. Anaximander (610–*c.*547 BCE), a student of Thales,

THALES OF MILETUS

Greek philosophers did not conduct experiments but studied the world around them. The founder of Greek philosophy, Thales (625–546 BCE), had many interests. Not only did he realize that water was essential to life, he also investigated cosmology and surveying. He studied the path of the Moon and gained great respect when, in 585 BCE, he predicted a solar eclipse accurately. Thales died when he fell off a cliff as he gazed at the stars.

THE ELEMENTS

Most Greek philosophers' theories of matter featured the idea of four basic substances called elements: fire, air, water, and earth. Anaximenes (570–500 BCE) believed air was the key element. He thought pressure turned air into water (below), then earth, and finally stone. Around 450 BCE, Empedocles (490–430 BCE) suggested all substances were blends of the four elements. Aristotle, who lived a century later, proposed a fifth element called ether.

THE BEGINNING OF ATOMS

The first person to propose the existence of atoms was the Greek philosopher Leucippus (c. 450–370 BCE). His student, Democritus (right), developed the idea when he suggested that matter was made of tiny indestructible particles that he called atoma, Greek for "uncuttables." Democritus believed that different kinds of atoms made different kinds of matter. He thought that smooth atoms formed liquids and jagged ones locked together as solids.

modified Thales's theory by suggesting the existence of a universal substance called apeiron. Apeiron was thought to contain all possible opposites, such as hot and cold, and wet and dry. According to the theory, a pebble might be a mixture of the cold, hard, and dry parts of apeiron. Other substances might be combinations of the hot, soft, and wet parts of apeiron.

In the fifth century BCE two philosophers proposed that matter consisted of atoms. Their theory was later sidelined when the famous philosopher Aristotle (384–322 BCE) returned to the theory of elements. Aristotle believed fire, air, water, and earth made up all matter on Earth, and that the sky and beyond were made of a fifth element called ether.

PRECIOUS AND BASE METALS

Gold (right) and silver occur naturally. They were very rare commodities until people learned to release pure metals from their ores (the raw state in which they occur in nature). Their rarity and shining beauty, combined with the ease with which they can be fashioned into coins, ornaments, and utensils, made gold and silver valued as precious metals. Lead is useful but was never considered precious. It is easy to extract lead from plentiful ores. The dark, dull metal is easily shaped, which makes it useful for practical applications such as plumbing and roofing. Lead tarnishes quickly and has less glamorous uses than silver or gold, so it is an example of a base metal.

No one knows exactly how alchemy began, but it is certain that people have worked with metals for many thousands of years. The ancient Chinese believed gold could make someone live longer. This belief drove their attempts to produce gold from base metals such as lead. Later alchemists tried to turn lead into gold to make money for themselves or their sponsors. Turning one substance into another was known as transmutation. Transmutation also applied to changing sickness to health and old age to youth. Alchemists sought ways to realize all these goals.

Alchemists often worked in secret and enacted rituals that combined ancient myths with religion and astrology. Alchemists used symbols, rhymes, and codes to protect their methods from competitors. Some alchemists reported success in making gold from less valuable substances, but the records of their methods are often impossible to understand. Chemists now know that no chemical reaction can make gold from another element. The alchemists who claimed they could make gold were bluffing or fooling themselves. By the late fourth century

BCE, alchemy had reached Alexandria, an Egyptian city near the mouth of the Nile River. Alexandrian alchemists adopted Aristotle's theory of the four earthly elements. The result was a new form of alchemy based on fire, air, water, and earth. Alexandrian alchemy later spread to Europe. Some renowned scientists, including Isaac Newton, were secret alchemists.

METALS AND PLANETS

The alchemists of the fourth century BCE linked each of the planets and the Sun and Moon with metals. Often the associations reflected the appearance of both items: The Sun was linked with gold, the Moon with silver, and the rust-colored planet Mars with iron. Other planets and many more metals have since been discovered.

Planet	Sun	Mercury	Venus	Moon	Mars	Jupiter	Saturn	Uranus	Neptune	Pluto
Metal	Gold	Mercury	Copper	Silver	Iron	Tin	Lead	None	None	None

Above: Alchemists associated the planets with metals, but their knowledge of heavenly bodies and chemical elements was far from complete. The outer planets—Uranus and Neptune—and the dwarf plant Pluto were unknown two thousand four hundred years ago.

2 THE ELEMENT DETECTIVES

In the late seventeenth century, chemists started to move away from alchemy. Their experiments became more thorough and accurate, and chemists soon began to understand more about the workings of matter.

THE ALCHEMISTS FAILED IN their quests to turn lead into gold and produce an elixir of life that would make people live forever.

Despite their questionable aims and methods, alchemists paved the way for modern chemistry by creating recipes for making useful chemicals

PHOSPHORUS

Hennig Brand thought he might get gold from urine because of their similar colors. He boiled urine down to a paste, mixed it with sand, and heated the mixture. The vapors cooled to give a waxy solid that glowed in air and sometimes caught fire. Brand called this material phosphorus, which is Greek for "bringer of light." Phosphorus is now extracted from rocks.

Phosphorus is a main ingredient in match heads.

ELEMENT

To an alchemist, the elements were fire, air, water, and earth. Modern chemists use the same word to describe the components of all substances. A chemical element cannot be separated into a simpler form by chemical processes. An element can be divided physically into atoms without altering its basic chemical properties (*see* page 21).

THE SKEPTICAL CHEMIST

In 1661 Irish-born Robert Boyle (1627–1691; right) wrote a book called *The Skeptical Chemist*. The word *chemist* was a shortened version of "alchemist" and caught on as the term for people who study chemicals. In his article, Boyle correctly proposed elements as the simplest forms of matter that could be detected by chemical tests. Boyle thought that gases consisted of small particles surrounded by space. This idea fit with the ancient Greek Democritus's atomic model of matter. When Boyle found that rusting metals gained weight, he realized correctly that particles in the metal were combining with particles in air.

such as alcohol, ammonia, and acids. Later chemists used these materials in their experiments. Alchemists also developed techniques for separating mixtures into individual substances.

Some alchemists' achievements were strokes of luck. In 1669 the German alchemist Hennig Brand discovered phosphorus by chance as he searched for gold in urine. People were amazed by phosphorus because it glowed in the dark and ignited. It was the first new element to be discovered for more than a century.

The discovery of phosphorus came a few years after Robert Boyle suggested there must be more elements than just fire, air, water, and earth. Alchemists thought smoke was a form of air. Boyle knew differently: He discovered that it was composed of soot, moisture, and tars.

THE CHAMPION OF PHLOGISTON

German scientist Georg Stahl (1660–1734) went to great lengths to defend his theory of phlogiston against critics. One of Stahl's suggestions was that the form of phlogiston lost during corrosion must have negative weight. He came up with this strange theory to explain why substances such as iron gain weight when they corrode.

RUST

The theory of phlogiston interrupted scientific progress. Robert Boyle had already proposed that rusting was the combination of iron with particles in the air. He was correct. Iron combines with oxygen from the air to produce the rough and reddish substance called rust, shown here magnified many times.

Robert Boyle's idea that particles of different substances combined during rusting was correct. Rusting is an example of a chemical reaction. Boyle reported his experiments in accurate detail, unlike the alchemists before him who guarded their secrets. Some historians hail Boyle as the first true chemist. After Boyle died, the development of chemistry into its modern form was hampered by a false theory. In 1703 Georg Stahl proposed the existence of phlogiston. He got the name from the Greek word phlogistos, meaning "inflammable." He believed burning and rusting were the same process at different speeds. Stahl thought that ashes or rust remained when all phlogiston had escaped from a material. Phlogiston theory persisted for more than a century. A number of scientists supported the theory through their own findings. In 1766 the British scientist Henry Cavendish (1731–1810) suggested that phlogiston was the inflammable air that forms when acids corrode metals. The idea seemed to make sense to Cavendish because it linked burning to corrosion. We now know inflammable air as hydrogen.

British chemist Joseph Priestley (1733–1804) isolated a gas from air in 1774. He noted that substances burned more brightly in the new gas than they did in air. Priestley concluded that the new gas was lacking in phlogiston and named it "dephlogisticated air."

Antoine-Laurent Lavoisier, a French chemist, destroyed phlogiston theory in 1777. He burned samples of sulfur

ANTOINE-LAURENT LAVOISIER

Lavoisier (right; holding flask) was born in Paris in 1743. As a youth he boasted that he was destined for glory. It was no exaggeration: The many discoveries he made have prompted some people to call him the father of modern chemistry. Lavoisier also became a very rich man. In later life Lavoisier used his chemical knowledge to improve farming methods and the manufacture of gunpowder. He also worked on tax reform. Rich people became very unpopular during the French Revolution. In 1794 revolutionaries executed Lavoisier by guillotine.

THE CALORIC THEORY

Scientists once believed that heat was caused by a mysterious invisible fluid called caloric. They thought that a piece of metal heats up when it is beaten with a hammer because hot caloric flows out of it. What really causes the heat is energy transferred from the hammer blows. Similarly, heat from exercise is not the release of caloric but heat energy released from working muscles (right).

COMPOUNDS

A compound is a substance made from two or more elements. Water (shown in the model below) is a compound of hydrogen and oxygen; ammonia is a compound of hydrogen and nitrogen. Compounds form when elements or other compounds join during a chemical reaction. The links that hold elements and compounds together are called chemical bonds.

and phosphorus and weighed the products. Lavoisier discovered that the products were heavier than the initial samples. The increase in weight came from the air. Lavoisier realized that the burning elements were not releasing phlogiston, but combining with the gas then called dephlogisticated air. Lavoisier renamed the gas oxygène (oxygen) after the Greek for "acid maker," because the products of

burning phosphorus and sulfur dissolved in water to form acids. Like Boyle, Lavoisier worked in an organized way and reported his work clearly. He discovered many chemical elements and made a list of thirty-three. Two were not elements—light and caloric, or heat. Eight were compounds that he failed to break down into their basic elements. The rest were true chemical elements.

By the end of the eighteenth century, chemists knew that common substances such as water were made from elements joined as compounds. Scientists proved this fact by breaking compounds apart into the chemical elements that made them up. In 1799 Humphry Davy (1778–1829) discovered that by passing an electrical current through some compounds in a process now called electrolysis, he could separate them into their component elements.

THE GAS MAN

British chemist Humphry Davy, shown here giving a lecture, is most famous for developing the Davy lamp. The lamp was a safety light for miners that replaced open flames such as candles. The Davy lamp did not ignite the explosive gases that often build up in coal mines. Davy's simple invention saved the lives of many hundreds of miners. A lifetime of breathing dangerous gases in his chemistry lab is believed to have cost Davy his own life. He became seriously ill in 1827 and died after a heart attack two years later.

DAVY DISCOVERS ELECTROLYSIS

Davy placed two pieces of metal called electrodes into a jar of water and wired them to a battery cell. As the electric current flowed between the electrodes, the water split into its two elements, hydrogen and oxygen, which were given off as gases. Davy used the same method to separate other substances and discovered new elements, including potassium and sodium. Using electricity to separate compounds became known as electrolysis.

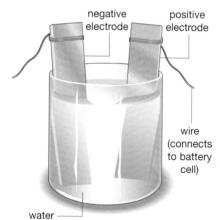

Passing a mild electric current through water can separate the liquid into hydrogen and oxygen.

3 ARRANGING THE ELEMENTS

Chemists such as Humphry Davy split many compounds into their component elements. Along the way, they discovered many new elements. Now chemists needed to find out how the elements related to one another.

SOME SCIENTISTS FOLLOWED Lavoisier and tried to understand elements by studying chemical reactions. In 1794, French chemist Joseph-Louis Proust (1754–1826) formulated his law of constant composition. The law states that the ratios of weights of elements in a

JOHN DALTON: FATHER OF ATOMIC THEORY

After many years of careful scientific research, English scientist John Dalton (1766–1844; right) devised the atomic theory of matter. This was one of the most important scientific theories of all time. Before Dalton, scientists thought that all atoms were the same. Dalton realized that each element had a different atom. He also suggested that all atoms of any one element had the same mass (amount of matter). Dalton's ideas were not entirely correct, but chemists continued to use them for much of the nineteenth century.

DALTON PICTURES THE ELEMENTS

John Dalton used circular symbols (below) to represent the different elements. Some years later, Swedish chemist Jöns Jakob Berzelius (1779–1848) developed the modern system of chemical symbols based on letters and numbers. The letters represented the elements, such as H for hydrogen. The numbers declared the ratios between the elements. Water is H_2O, which explains that two parts of hydrogen (H_2) combine with one part of oxygen (0) to form water.

ELEMENTS

				wt.
⊙	Hydrogen	1	⊕ Strontian	46
⊖	Azote	5	✦ Barytes	68
⬤	Carbon	5½	Ⓘ Iron	50
○	Oxygen	7	Ⓩ Zinc	56
⊗	Phosphorus	9	Ⓒ Copper	56
⊕	Sulphur	13	Ⓛ Lead	90
⊘	Magnesia	20	Ⓢ Silver	190
⊖	Lime	24	ⓖ Gold	190
⊜	Soda	28	Ⓟ Platina	190
⫴	Potash	42	✹ Mercury	167

DALTON VERSUS GAY-LUSSAC

The work of Gay-Lussac (right) suggested Dalton's ideas were incomplete or wrong. Dalton saw this as a threat to his new atomic theory and did his best to discredit Gay-Lussac. Dalton claimed Gay-Lussac's measurements were poor and said he could not "admit the French doctrine" and accept Gay-Lussac's ideas.

compound are always the same. For example, hydrogen and oxygen always join in the same proportions to form water. British scientist John Dalton realized that the proportions of elements in a compound would be the same if each element consisted of particles, or atoms, with a fixed size and mass. Dalton published his theory in 1803, together with a list of atomic masses for twelve elements. Dalton

believed that simple compounds formed when one particle of each element joined to make one particle of the final product. Frenchman Joseph Louis Gay-Lussac (1778–1850) disagreed. In 1809 he found that when two gases react together, the ratio of elements in the resulting compound varies depending on which gases are involved. For example, two volumes of hydrogen gas combine with one volume

AMEDEO AVOGADRO

Amedeo Avogadro (1776–1856; right) was one of the greatest chemists of his time but others, including Dalton and Gay-Lussac, did not accept his theories. Avogadro's work fell into disfavor. Only after he was dead did scientists come to realize the true significance of Avogadro's groundbreaking work.

of oxygen gas to make two volumes of water. This puzzled Dalton. He could not see how three particles of hydrogen and oxygen could form two of water.

In 1811 Amedeo Avogadro realized that Dalton had confused the idea of an atom with that of a molecule. Dalton knew that an atom is the smallest possible amount of an element. He did not realize that atoms of some elements join with themselves to form molecules. Dalton thought that one atom of hydrogen and one

SPLITTING THE MOLECULE?

A molecule is the smallest possible amount of a compound. It cannot be split without breaking up the molecule into its constituent chemical elements. If you take a glass of water and throw half away, that leaves half a glass of water. If you divide it in two again and again, you end up with half the amount of water each time, but the substance is still water. Eventually there comes a point when there is one molecule (right) of water left. To reduce the amount of water further would involve breaking the water molecule into its component hydrogen and oxygen atoms. At that point the substance is no longer the compound water, it is hydrogen and oxygen. Elements can also join with themselves and make molecules. For example, a single molecule of oxygen gas is formed by two atoms of oxygen.

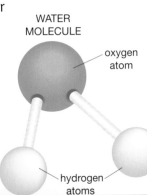

WATER MOLECULE

oxygen atom

hydrogen atoms

AVOGADRO'S LAW

Avogadro wondered what would happen if he took large empty jars and filled them up with different gases at the same temperature and pressure. He realized that at the same volume, temperature, and pressure, all gases would always contain equal numbers of molecules. The principle applied no matter what gases he put in the jars. It became known as Avogadro's law.

AVOGADRO'S NUMBER

Avogadro knew the number of molecules would be equal at the same volume, temperature, and pressure for any gas, but he could not know how many molecules that was because his equipment was nowhere near sensitive enough. Scientists later found that the number of molecules in two grams of hydrogen is around 600,000,000,000,000,000,000,000. This huge number became known as Avogadro's number. It is such a large number that it is almost impossible to picture. If the entire surface of the United States were covered in grains of sand to a depth of about six feet (two meters), the number of sand grains would be similar to Avogadro's number. If a machine started to count the sand grains at a rate of one per second, it would take 20,000 trillion years to reach Avogadro's number.

atom of oxygen combined to form one particle of the compound water. Avogadro discovered that one molecule of two oxygen atoms combined with two molecules of two hydrogen atoms to make two parts of water. He was the first person to realize the crucial difference between an atom and a molecule. Amadeo Avogadro's other discoveries include Avogadro's law. This law states that equal volumes of different gases at the same temperature and pressure always contain the same number of molecules. The weight varies between different gases, but the number of molecules is always the same. It became known as Avogadro's number.

RELATIVE ATOMIC MASS

Atoms and molecules are extremely small. Measuring the mass of a single molecule or atom involves working with tiny numbers and using sensitive equipment. An easier way is to compare the mass of atoms with a known amount: Scientists currently use a system based on one-twelfth of the mass of a carbon atom. This makes the relative atomic mass of a hydrogen atom, the smallest atom, 1. Helium, the next smallest atom, is 4 times as heavy as hydrogen and is given a relative atomic mass of 4. One atom of uranium is around 238 times as heavy as a hydrogen atom, and its atomic mass is 238.

MENDELEYEV

Mendeleyev set out a table of elements in order of their increasing relative atomic mass. He started with hydrogen, the smallest. Next he cut the list into rows and stacked similar elements together in columns. Mendeleyev had produced the first periodic table using rows, or periods, and columns, or groups of elements.

Avogadro's work gave scientists a good idea of the number of atoms or molecules contained in everyday amounts of common substances. According to Avogadro's number, 0.4 ounces (12 g) of the most common form of carbon holds more than six hundred thousand million million million carbon atoms (600, 000, 000, 000, 000, 000, 000, 000). Avogadro's work was neglected until another Italian, Stanislao Cannizzaro (1826–1910), revived his ideas. Cannizzaro realized that Avogadro's law could be applied to compare the mass of different atoms and molecules. This idea was called relative atomic mass. Relative atomic mass was a simple way of comparing different elements and it revolutionized chemistry.

Chemical knowledge was growing fast. By the 1860s, chemists had discovered sixty-three chemical elements. They wondered what these elements had in common and how they were related to one another. Russian chemist Dmitri Mendeleyev (1834–1907) solved the puzzle in 1869. He compared the properties of different elements and came up with the periodic table. There were gaps in the original table, but Mendeleyev was confident enough to not only claim that the gaps would be filled when chemists discovered new elements but also to predict the chemical properties of the unknown elements. Later scientists proved Mendeleyev was right.

THE PERIODIC TABLE

The periodic table has been updated many time since Mendeleyev's time. Newly discovered elements were added and the positions of some elements were moved around as chemists learned more about the elements and their properties.

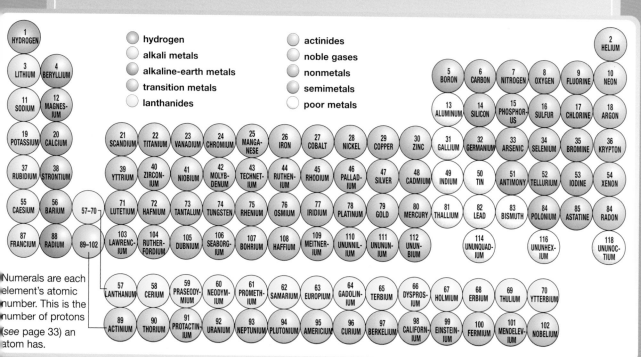

Numerals are each element's atomic number. This is the number of protons (see page 33) an atom has.

4 INVESTIGATING HOW MOLECULES BEHAVE

Avogadro's law helped chemists think in terms of molecules, but they still did not know how molecules behave and how they are arranged. Understanding the behavior and arrangement of molecules was the crucial next step.

KINETIC THEORY ANSWERED many puzzles for chemists. It was developed in the nineteenth century from Avogadro's ideas by a brilliant group of scientists, notably British physicist James Clerk Maxwell (1831–1879) and Austrian physicist Ludwig Boltzmann (1844–1906).

LUDWIG BOLTZMANN

Ludwig Boltzmann (below) moved frequently from one university job to another. Boltzmann suffered from an illness called bipolar disorder. His condition caused his moods to swing back and forth from wild happiness and action to great despair and inactivity. Boltzmann killed himself in 1906, at the age of sixty-two, possibly because he feared his theories on kinetics were about to be proved wrong. After Boltzmann's death, his ideas were accepted as being among the most important contributions to twentieth-century chemistry and physics.

KINETIC THEORY

Kinetic theory is the study of the movements of molecules. Molecules in all substances move about. In solids they vibrate in position, and in gases they whiz around freely. How much they move depends on the temperature. The molecules vibrate or move around more when a substance heats up. Kinetic theory also links heat and pressure. The pressure of a gas is due to collisions between the molecules and the container walls. The higher the temperature, the greater the speed of the molecules. Speedier molecules are more likely to hit the walls more often. More collisions mean more pressure.

THERMODYNAMICS

Chemical reactions often cause heating or cooling. Thermodynamics explains how heat energy is taken in or released during a chemical reaction. More than just a theory, thermodynamics has many practical uses. These include working out how to make chemical reactions happen more easily and calculating how to make engines more efficient by converting more fuel into useful power (right).

Kinetic theory made an important connection between chemistry and physics. *Kinetic* is a word that means movement. The theory explains why substances behave as they do by looking at the physics of how molecules move. Kinetic theory explains that gases behave as they do because their molecules are moving about constantly. The theory also led to the science called thermodynamics, which means "heat in motion." Kinetic theory also explains how gases always expand to fill as much space, or volume, as they can. The moving gas molecules stop spreading out only when they hit a barrier, such as the side of a container. If the molecules of all substances were completely free to move about, they would all be gases.

FORCES

A force is a pushing or pulling action. Magnetism is an example of a force. A magnet can pull pieces of metal toward it, as with the iron filings in this photo. A magnet can also attract or repel (push away) other magnets. The forces inside chemicals work in a similar way to magnetism, but they act on the scale of atoms and molecules.

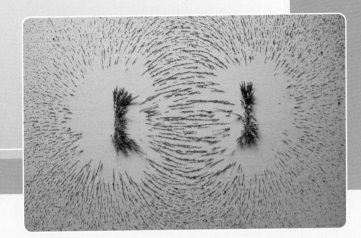

Gases expand to fill any available space, but solids and liquids do not. There must be some force that holds the molecules together more closely in liquids and solids than in gases. Many substances, such as salts and metals, are solids in which the molecules are held together very tightly. They have a regular crystal structure that prevents the molecules from moving around as much as they do in gases and liquids. In less structured solids and in liquids, the molecules are arranged more loosely and held together by weaker bonds. The weak forces that hold together liquids and noncrystalline solids are named van der Waals forces for their discoverer, Johannes Diderik van der Waals.

JOHANNES DIDERIK VAN DER WAALS

When former Dutch schoolteacher Johannes Diderik van der Waals (1837–1923; right) published his first scientific results, the distinguished British physicist James Clerk Maxwell was impressed. Maxwell commented: "There can be no doubt that the name of Van der Waals will soon be among the foremost in molecular science." Maxwell was right. Van der Waals became the outstanding physicist of his day and won the prestigious Nobel Prize for physics in 1910.

Van der Waals helped to show that solids, liquids, and gases are all versions of fundamentally the same thing. For example, steam, water, and ice are all forms of water, but they behave in different ways due to the forces between the molecules. Van der Waals helped extend the kinetic theory by showing how the pressure, volume, and temperature of ordinary gases were linked by simple math.

SOLIDS, LIQUIDS, AND GASES

The molecules in a solid are fixed loosely in place. They vibrate but do not move around widely. Molecular forces such as van der Waals forces keep the molecules in position. When a solid such as ice is heated, the molecules gain energy and vibrate more energetically. Eventually the heat gives the molecules enough energy to overcome the molecular forces. When the forces can no longer hold the molecules in place, they start to move more freely. The solid ice melts into liquid water. If the liquid is heated further, the molecules move about more freely still and the liquid vaporizes into a gas.

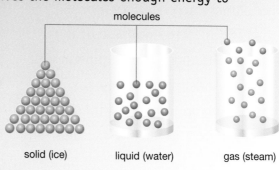

molecules

solid (ice)   liquid (water)   gas (steam)

VALENCY

Chemical bonds hold molecules in compounds together. The valency of an atom explains how many bonds, or links, it can form with other atoms to make compounds. Water has the chemical symbol H_2O, which shows that two hydrogen atoms link up with a single oxygen atom (below). In each molecule of water, two hydrogen atoms link to a single oxygen atom. The valency of hydrogen is one, so each hydrogen atom can link to only one other atom. Oxygen has a valency of two, so each oxygen atom can link to two other atoms. Different elements have a different valency. Carbon has a valency of four, which means it can make links with up to four other atoms.

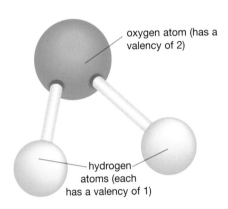

oxygen atom (has a valency of 2)

hydrogen atoms (each has a valency of 1)

Van der Waals forces are weak links between molecules. The chemical bonds that lock atoms together in molecules involve much stronger forces. American chemist Gilbert Lewis (1875–1946) was one of the scientists who did most to explain chemical bonds. He played a key role in developing an important theory called valency. This theory explains why elements join in different proportions to form compounds. Valency advances and explains the ideas put forward earlier by both Dalton and Gay-Lussac.

The theory of valency had another important impact. A German chemist named Friedrich Kekulé (1829–1896) found that carbon always has a valency of four. This discovery led him to make a number of important discoveries about the chemistry of carbon and also formulate a famous theory about benzene. Most important of all, Kekulé found that carbon could link into very long and complicated chains.

Carbon chemistry is important because carbon is the basis for all living things. By 1900, Kekulé's work had spawned the new field of chemistry called organic chemistry.

This paved the way for two of the most important scientific discoveries of the twentieth century: photosynthesis, or how plants make food from sunlight, and the structure of DNA, the genetic (inherited) material in the cells of living things.

ORGANIC CHEMISTRY

Organic chemistry is the study of carbon and its compounds. In the twentieth century, organic chemistry proved to be one of the most important and far-reaching branches of chemistry. Organic chemistry is crucial to such important industrial applications as oil refining. It is also used in the manufacture of plastics (below). Plastics are formed by long chains of carbon-based molecules called polymers.

BENZENE RING

Benzene is used in the manufacture of many products, from explosives to nylon and plastics to antiseptics. Kekulé was the first person to realize that the structure of a molecule of benzene is based on a ring of six carbon atoms (below; gray). He said the idea came to him when he dreamed about a snake, coiled into a circle, biting its own tail.

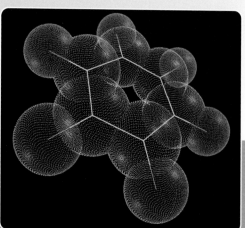

5 THE ATOM'S STRUCTURE

Molecules form when atoms combine. But what forms atoms? Toward the end of the nineteenth century, the discovery of radioactivity led to scientists' first real glimpse inside the atom.

WHILE SOME SCIENTISTS sought to better understand the mysteries of molecules, others were probing deeper into the atom. The word atom once meant something that could not be split. A series of important discoveries by scientists in the late nineteenth century suggested the idea of the indivisible atom was too simple. New discoveries gave

RADIOACTIVITY

Most elements have stable atoms that are held together effectively by strong bonds. Some elements are less stable. Unstable elements, such as uranium, give off radioactivity. Radioactivity is tiny energetic particles that fire out from an atom at great speed. The particles can be detected by a Geiger counter (below). When the atom has given off all its radioactive particles, it becomes stable, or nonradioactive.

MARIE CURIE

Marie Curie (below) was born in Poland in 1867. She moved to Paris and started to work with radioactivity around her thirtieth birthday. No one then knew about the dangers of radioactivity. Curie died in 1934 from leukemia, a cancer of the blood. Her illness was most likely caused by years of exposure to radiation through her work. Radiation has since been used by doctors to kill cancerous cells and has helped extend the lives of millions of people.

TINY AMOUNTS

Radioactive elements decay (change naturally) into other materials, so they are often very hard to find. It took the Curies four years of hard work to extract a few hundredths of an ounce (about 1 g) of radioactive radium chloride from a colossal 9 tons (8.8 metric tons) of uranium ore (left), which is called pitchblende.

scientists new insights into the fascinating structure of atoms.

Radioactivity was discovered accidentally in 1896. French physicist Antoine Henri Becquerel (1852–1908) chanced upon radioactivity when he left a lump of uranium ore, called pitchblende, on top of a photographic plate. Radioactivity from the uranium caused a ghostly image of the pitchblende to appear on the photographic plate. The following year, a young French physicist named Marie Curie began to explore radiation. Curie and her husband, Pierre, processed huge amounts of ore to extract tiny amounts of radioactive materials for her to study. Curie discovered two new radioactive elements: polonium (which was named for Poland, the country where she was born) and radium.

RUTHERFORD'S RECOGNITION

New Zealand-born physicist Ernest Rutherford (1871–1937; right) performed most of his famous experiments on atoms and radioactivity while he worked at Cambridge University in England. The importance of his work was recognized in many ways. Rutherford won the Nobel Prize for physics in 1908, and the king of England knighted him Sir Ernest Rutherford in 1914. When Rutherford died in 1937, he was buried in Westminster Abbey, London, alongside Sir Isaac Newton, Charles Darwin, and the kings and queens of England.

Thanks to the work of Ernest Rutherford and his colleagues, the study of radioactivity soon began to provide insights into the structure of the atom. If radioactive atoms gave off particles, then atoms must be built from smaller particles. When unstable atoms change into stable ones, some of these particles are thrown out. It was these particles that scientists such as Marie Curie had detected being given off by radioactive substances. By 1900, Rutherford had discovered that there were three different types of radiation. In 1911 Rutherford carried out a famous experiment when he fired radiation at a very thin piece of gold foil. The results of this experiment led Rutherford to suggest the theory of the nuclear atom, or the idea that every atom has a dense positively charged nucleus at its center, surrounded by space.

RUTHERFORD'S GOLD FOIL EXPERIMENT

Rutherford and his assistant Ernest Marsden fired alpha particles at thin gold foil. Most of the alpha particles passed right through, as Rutherford had expected, but some bounced straight back. Rutherford said: "It was as though you had fired a fifteen-inch shell at a piece of tissue paper and it had bounced back and hit you." Alpha particles have a positive charge. They would bounce back only if the atoms in the gold foil also contained a large concentrated positive charge.

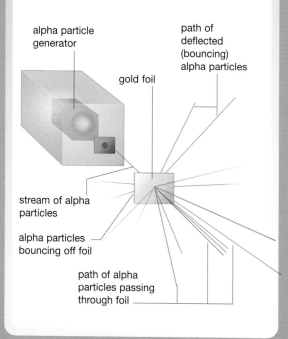

TYPES OF RADIATION

Rutherford discovered three types of radiation given off by atoms: alpha particles, beta particles, and gamma rays. An alpha particle has the same structure as the nucleus of a helium atom. It consists of two protons (particles with a positive electrical charge) and two neutrons (particles with no charge). A beta particle is the same thing as an electron (a particle with a negative charge). It is smaller and travels faster and farther than an alpha particle. Gamma rays are similar to X-rays, radio waves, and other kinds of electromagnetic radiation. Gamma rays travel long distances and pass right through solid objects.

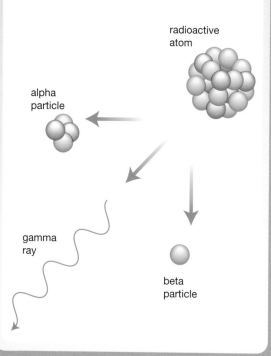

RUTHERFORD THE ALCHEMIST?

Ernest Rutherford proved it was possible to change one element into another by splitting the atom. He fired alpha particles at nitrogen atoms. The particles split some of the nitrogen atoms into smaller hydrogen and oxygen atoms. Rutherford's aims and methods differed from those of the alchemists, but by changing one element into another, he achieved their goal of transmutation. The vital difference was his approach: Alchemists tried to change elements using chemical reactions; Rutherford split nitrogen atoms physically by firing particles at them.

J.J. THOMSON

J.J. Thomson is remembered most for his discovery of the electron in 1897. It was his most startling discovery. Thomson taught at Cambridge University, England, where he worked with Ernest Rutherford. Thomson had once championed the plum pudding theory of atomic structure (below). It was while working with Thomson that Rutherford disproved the plum pudding theory by performing his gold foil experiment.

A few years before Rutherford's famous gold foil experiment, British physicist J.J. Thomson (1856–1940), discovered a new particle. It became known as the electron. Electrons are far smaller than atoms and carry tiny amounts of negative charge. Thomson wondered where electrons fit into the atom. He believed that atoms were made up like plum puddings. The electrons were "plums" dotted randomly inside a much larger mass of positive matter, the "pudding."

Rutherford's gold foil experiment proved that Thomson's picture of the atom was wrong. The positive matter in an atom had to be concentrated in its center, not scattered throughout the atom. With Rutherford's help, Danish physicist Niels Bohr (1885–1962) put together a new picture of the atom in 1913. Far from being uncuttable, as the original meaning of the word atom suggested, atoms seemed to be built from three kinds of smaller particles. Atoms were not, after all, the basic building blocks of matter. Inside an atom were subatomic particles called electrons, protons, and neutrons. In Bohr's model of the atom, a central nucleus held the protons and neutrons while electrons whizzed around the outer space of the atom.

THE BOHR MODEL OF SUBATOMIC PARTICLES

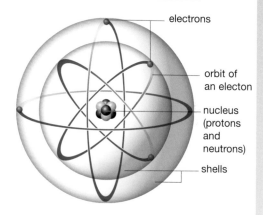

electrons

orbit of an electon

nucleus (protons and neutrons)

shells

ELECTRONS

If atoms are small, then electrons are almost unimaginably tiny. Even the smallest atoms are more than a thousand times the size of an electron. If it were possible to scale up an electron so it weighed as much as an apple, and an apple could be scaled up by the same amount, the resulting apple would weigh about one million times as much as Earth.

Atoms are composed of three types of subatomic particles: protons, neutrons, and electrons. There are approximately the same number of protons and neutrons in an atom, and there are exactly the same number of protons as electrons. Protons and neutrons form the central core of an atom, called the nucleus. Protons are positively charged, neutrons have no charge, and electrons are negatively charged. Protons and neutrons clump together tightly in the nucleus. Much of the rest of an atom is empty space. According to the Bohr model (above), electrons move around the nucleus a little like planets orbit the Sun. During their orbit, electrons occupy defined areas called shells.

6 FUTURE PROSPECTS

Scientists may never form a complete understanding of atoms and molecules, but they have learned enough to develop many practical technologies from the theories of atomic physics.

ALMOST A CENTURY AFTER Rutherford's famous experiments, the picture of the atom is still not complete. In 1913 Bohr put forward the idea that electrons moved in orbits around the nucleus. This theory proved to be too simple. In the 1920s, a set of new ideas called quantum theory suggested that electrons did not always behave like particles. Sometimes they act as waves and spread out like a fuzzy cloud.

QUANTUM THEORY

Quantum theory is an attempt to explain the mysterious world inside the atom. The theory is based on the idea that energy exists in fixed-sized packets called quanta. A single packet of energy is called a quantum. One of the ideas behind quantum theory is that electrons behave sometimes as particles and at other times like a wave.

PARTICLE ACCELERATORS

A particle accelerator is a bit like an immensely long cannon. Instead of shooting shells, it uses huge amounts of energy to fire subatomic particles at each other. When the particles collide, they explode in a shower of smaller particles.

MURRAY GELL-MANN

Murray Gell-Mann (1929–) won the 1969 Nobel Prize for physics (below, on right) for his quark theory. Gell-Mann believes a great scientist must have two qualities. He calls these qualities "good taste" and "killer instinct." Good taste means picking the right problems to work on. The killer instinct involves pursuing ideas with utter determination.

QUARKS

Scientists theorize that quarks are the basic particles from which protons and neutrons are made. There are six types of quarks and they have rather unusual names: top, bottom, up, down, charm, and strange. No one has yet seen a quark, but experiments and theories suggest they must exist.

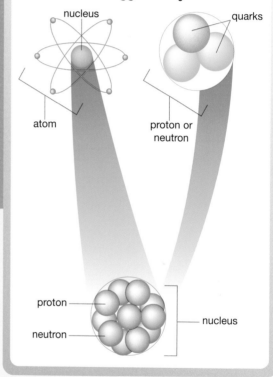

nucleus

quarks

atom

proton or neutron

proton

neutron

nucleus

As scientists gained a greater understanding of the atom, they realized that its structure was more complex than they had thought previously. Particle accelerators helped physicists discover new particles inside the atom.

In the 1960s, the American physicists Murray Gell-Mann (born 1929) and George Zweig (born 1937) proposed that protons and neutrons are each composed of more fundamental particles, which they called quarks. Protons and neutrons are made up of quarks, but whether quarks really are the basic building blocks of matter remains to be proven.

The twentieth century was often called the atomic age. Scientists still had questions about the structure of atoms, but they knew enough to put them to productive use. Studies by scientists such as Ernest Rutherford and Marie Curie led to the idea that atoms would give off massive amounts of energy when they broke apart. The most spectacular demonstration of this was the invention of the atomic bomb during World War II (1939–1945). People later harnessed the power of atoms for peaceful purposes. The first atomic power plants to produce electricity were built in the 1950s.

ATOMIC BOMB

Some radioactive atoms decay by splitting into smaller, more stable atoms, and release a burst of energy as they do so. Under certain conditions, a single reaction sets off a chain of other reactions. The chain reaction generates a colossal amount of energy that provides the huge explosive power of an atomic bomb. Just 2.2 pounds (1 kg) of uranium can make an explosion like that produced by 17,000 tons (17,270 metric tons) of conventional explosive.

CHERNOBYL CONTROVERSY

At first, people heralded nuclear power as the fuel of the future. Dirty coal-fired power stations could be replaced with seemingly clean nuclear reactors. The image of nuclear power was tarnished, however, by accidents and leaks, such as one in 1979 at Three Mile Island, Pennsylvania (above). Even greater realization of the risks of radioactivity came in 1986 when the world's worst nuclear accident hit the Chernobyl power plant in Ukraine. A cloud of radioactive gas covered much of Europe. Livestock was affected as far away as northern Europe. An unknown number of people in Ukraine and surrounding areas died of radiation-induced illnesses such as cancer.

The twenty-first century may prove to be the age of the molecule. Scientists once had to rely on searching for useful substances in nature, usually by accident. Now they use computers to design whole new molecules. Drugs are designed from scratch to have the right properties to cure particular diseases. Strong and lightweight materials engineered for cutting-edge applications such as space technology and deep-sea exploration can also be exploited for regular use.

Chemists are today at the forefront of technology that uses molecules in entirely new and exciting ways. One such important new field is the science of nanotechnology. The study of atoms and molecules has come a long way, but it is far from over.

NANOTECHNOLOGY

Nanotechnology involves building microscopic structures from atoms and molecules. One intriguing use might be to make miniature machines that travel inside the human body to carry out ultraprecise operations. Nanomachines like this could be built from tiny pieces called nanotubes (below). Nanotubes are sheets of carbon rolled into cylinders just a few nanometers across. One nanometer is about one-thousandth the width of a human hair. The cylinders can be joined together to make a nanomachine.

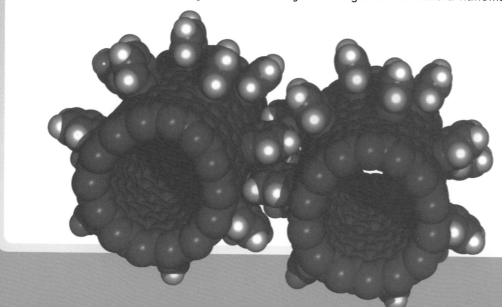

MAKING AN INDICATOR

GOALS

1. Make your own indicator solution.
2. Use the indicator to test liquids to see if they are acidic, neutral, or basic.

WHAT YOU WILL NEED

- red cabbage
- stainless steel or enamel pan or microwave casserole dish
- 1 quart (0.9l) water
- stove, microwave, or hot plate
- knife and cutting board
- measuring cup
- strainer
- vinegar and baking soda
- teaspoon
- 2 jars

1 Chop up the cabbage. Put the chopped cabbage in a covered pot with the water, and boil it for 30 minutes.

! **SAFETY TIP** *Be careful when using hot water and knives. Always have an adult present to supervise and to help you.*

2 After the cabbage water has cooled, strain it into a cup.

3 Pour ¼ cup of cabbage juice into a jar. Add ½ teaspoon baking soda to the jar and stir. Note what color the water turns.

4 Pour ¼ cup of cabbage juice into a jar, then add ½ teaspoon vinegar. Now what color does the water turn?

TROUBLESHOOTING

What if the indicator does not change color?

If you are testing a liquid that is a dark color, such as grape juice, it will be difficult to see the color change. This type of indicator only works well with clear or light-colored liquids and dissolved powders.

ACID RAIN

All rainwater is slightly acidic because carbon dioxide in the air dissolves in rain to form carbonic acid. Too much acid in rain damages plants, animals, and buildings. When fossil fuels like coal and oil are burned, they release acidic gases into the air that dissolve in water in the clouds to make strong acids. They then fall to the ground as acid rain.

5 Now pour the contents of the vinegar jar into the baking soda jar, and observe what happens.

TIMELINE

Atoms and Molecules	**2500 BCE** Tin ore is smelted in Turkey **4th century BCE** Greek philosopher Democritus believes the world is composed of tiny particles that cannot be divided	**1450** European metalworkers work out how to separate lead and silver ores
Electricity	**271 CE** The compass is first used in China; it works by detecting Earth's magnetic field	**1180** The first reference to the magnetic compass in Western writing is in Alexander Neckam's *Concerning Natural Things (De Naturis Rerum)*
Evolution		
Genetics		
Geology	**500 BCE** Xenophanes of Colphon (Greece) discovers that land can rise when he finds fossils of seashells on mountaintops	**1517** The Italian scientist Girolamo Fracastoro suggests that fossils are the remains of long-dead plants and animals
Gravity	**1450 BCE** Egyptians devise a water clock, based on the principle of dripping water **330 BCE** Aristotle believes that the Sun and planets orbit Earth	**1345** Dutch engineers use windmills to pump water out of areas that are being reclaimed from the sea
Light	**6000 BCE** People in Italy make mirrors from a rock called obsidian **1361 BCE** Chinese astronomers record a solar eclipse	**1021** Arab mathematician Alhazen writes about the refraction of light **1304** Theodoric of Freibourg, a German scientist, works out how rainbows form
Medicine	**2500 BCE** Chinese doctors begin using a pain-killing technique called acupuncture **1550 BCE** Egyptians are using about 700 drugs and medications	**365** Mechanical cranks are used to set broken bones in Greece **850** An Arab physician writes about eye disorders and treatments
Context	**c.3500 BCE** The wheel is invented in Mesopotamia **2630 BCE** Egyptians begin building the pyramids **776 BCE** The first Olympic Games are held in Greece **117 CE** Roman Empire reaches its greatest extent	**c.900** Mayan civilization in Mesoamerica collapses **1453** The Byzantine age comes to an end with the fall of Constantinople

6000 BCE   **300 CE**

1709 A model hot-air balloon is made in Brazil
1714 Gabriel Fahrenheit constructs a mercury thermometer

1738 Daniel Bernoulli proposes a kinetic theory of gases
c.1787 French physicist Jacques Charles draws up Charles's Law of gas volumes

1701 Edmond Halley draws up a map of Earth's magnetic field
1729 Stephen Gray explains electrical conductors and insulators

1742 Benjamin Franklin demonstrates the electrical nature of lightning
1800 Alessandro Volta develops the voltaic pile electric battery

1807 Humphry Davy uses electrolysis to isolate potassium and sodium
1822 André-Marie Ampere works out the laws of the movement of electricity

1650 Irish archbishop James Ussher mistakenly calculates that Earth was created in 4004 BCE

1809 Lamarck wrongly states that characteristics acquired during life are inherited by offspring
1831–36 Charles Darwin on HMS *Beagle*

1760s Robert Bakewell improves farmstock by selectively breeding animals

1831 Robert Brown is the first scientist to describe a cell nucleus

1691 Naturalist John Ray believes fossils are ancient life-forms

1793 Mammoth remains are found in Siberian permafrost

1811 Schoolgirl Mary Anning discovers the first fossil ichthyosaur
1815 Eruption of Mount Tambora in Indonesia modifies climates worldwide

1609 Johannes Kepler draws up laws of planetary motion
c.1665 Isaac Newton formulates his law of gravity

1665 Robert Hooke proposes that light travels in waves
1671 Isaac Newton shows that a prism splits light into a spectrum

1811 William Wollaston invents the *camera lucida*
1839 Louis Daguerre invents a kind of photograph taken on metal plates

1628 Physician William Harvey explains the circulation of blood
1721 Smallpox inoculation is carried out in North America

1745 The French surgeon Jacques Daviel successfully removes a cataract from a patient's eye—the first time this has happened

1805 Japanese physician Seishu Hoanoka performs surgery with general anesthesia
1811 Charles Bell pioneers study of the nervous system

1630 English Puritans colonize Massachusetts Bay
1665 Bubonic plague kills one-fifth of London's population

1787 The United States Constitution is adopted
1789 The French Revolution begins with the storming of the Bastille

1803 The Louisiana Purchase doubles the size of the United States
1833 A law is passed in Britain to abolish slavery in the British Empire

1600　　　　　　　**1730**　　　　　　　**1800**　　　　　　　**1850**

TIMELINE

	1850	1900
Atoms and Molecules	**1892** James Dewar invents the vacuum bottle **1896** Henri Becquerel discovers radioactivity **1897** Physicist J.J. Thompson is the first person to identify electrons	**1905** Albert Einstein publishes his special theory of relativity **1910** The existence of the nucleus of an atom is proven by Ernest Rutherford
Electricity	**1877** American engineer Thomas Edison invents the phonograph **1885** American electrical engineer William Stanley makes the first transformer	**1923** John Logie Baird makes a type of television
Evolution	**1856** Male Neanderthal skeleton found; it differs in important ways from modern human skeletons **1859** Charles Darwin publishes *On the Origin of Species*, arguing his case for evolution	**1908** Marcellin Boule reconstructs a skeleton of a Neanderthal person **1938** A coelanth "living fossil" is found in the ocean off the South African coast
Genetics	**1865** Gregor Mendel, an Austrian monk, puts forward his laws of inheritance; they are published the following year	**1909** Danish botanist Wilhelm Johannsen defines a gene **1913** Chromosome mapping is pioneered by Alfred Sturtevant
Geology	**1861** The first fossil *Archaeopteryx* is found **1883** Mount Krakatoa, in Indonesia, erupts; it is one of the largest volcanic eruptions in recorded history	**1913** Earth's age is calculated at 4.6 billion years by geologist Arthur Holmes **1935** Richter scale proposed to measure earthquake intensity
Gravity	**1851** Léon Foucault builds a pendulum (Foucault's pendulum) that shows Earth's rotation. **1891** John Poynting, an English physicist, works out the value of the gravitational constant	**1927** Georges Lemaitre suggests the universe originated with a "big bang"
Light	**1877** Joseph Swan, an English physicist, develops the first electric light bulb **1882** Albert Michelson calculates the speed of light to within 0.02 percent of the correct value	**1905** Albert Einstein publishes his special theory of relativity **1935** Transparency film invented by American amateur photographers
Medicine	**1885** Louis Pasteur manufactures a rabies vaccine **1898** The cause of malaria, the protozoa *Plasmodium*, is discovered by physician Ronald Ross **1903** X-rays first used to treat cancerous tumors	**1929** Hormone estrogen first isolated **1934** Radio waves used to treat cancer **1943** Kidney dialysis machine built by Willem Kolff
Context	**1861–1865** American Civil War **1876** The Sioux Army of Sitting Bull defeats U.S. forces at the Battle of Little Bighorn **1897** The Klondike Gold Rush begins	**1901** Guglielmo Marconi makes the first transatlantic radio broadcast **1914–1918** World War I **1939–1945** World War II

1952 The first hydrogen bomb is exploded on an atoll in the central Pacific
1960 First optical identification of a quasar
1967 Domestic microwave ovens are sold in U.S.

1994 American scientists discover a subatomic particle that they call the top quark
2004 A "supersolid" is discovered by American scientists—it flows through another material without friction

1961 The first silicon chips are manufactured
1962 The first national live TV broadcast, a speech by President Truman in San Francisco
1975 First commercial personal computers sold

1990 Work begins on developing the World Wide Web
2007 American scientists create flexible batteries by weaving microscopic tubes of carbon into paper

1960 Remains of human ancestor *Homo habilis* discovered in Tanzania
1983 Fossils of a 16-million-year-old ancestor of humans are found by Meave Leakey in Africa

1993 The oldest-known human ancestor, *Ardipithecus ramidus*, is discovered by Berkeley scientists
2003 Footprints of an upright-walking human, who was alive 350,000 years ago, are found in Italy

1953 The structure of DNA is discovered by Francis Crick and James Watson
1959 Down syndrome discovered to be caused by an extra chromosome

1994 The first genetically modifed tomato is sold in the U.S.
1996 A sheep named Dolly is cloned in Edinburgh
1998 Human stem cells are grown in a laboratory
2000 Human genome is roughly mapped out

1977 Frozen body of a baby mammoth found in Siberian permafrost

1996 Signs of microscopic life are found in a meteorite that originated from Mars
1997 Fossils of *Protarchaeopteryx*, a birdlike reptile, are found
2000 The fossil remains of a dinosaur's heart are found

1957 The first satellites, Sputnik 1 and Sputnik 2, are sent into orbit around Earth by the Soviet Union
1969 Astronauts Armstrong and Aldrin "bounce" on the Moon's surface, showing that gravity is less there

1992 Scientists at the University of Pisa, Italy, make the most accurate calculation of the acceleration due to gravity

1955 Indian scientist Narinder Kapany invents optical fibers for carrying light long distances
1962 Light-emitting diode (LED) invented

1998 Lasers are first used by American dentists for drilling teeth
2005 Flashes of light are discovered to create X-rays

1950 Link between smoking and lung cancer found
1958 Ultrasound scans are introduced to examine unborn babies
1967 The first successful heart transplant

1983 The human immunodeficiency virus (HIV) is discovered
1987 The first heart-lung-liver transplant is carried out by a team of British surgeons
2000 Works begins on making the first artificial heart

1955–1975 Vietnam War
1968 Martin Luther King assassinated in Memphis
1969 Neil Armstrong and Buzz Aldrin are the first people to walk on the Moon's surface

1989 Communist regimes across Europe collapse
1997 Diana, Princess of Wales, killed in a car accident in Paris
2001 Attack on the World Trade Center in New York
2008 Barack Obama elected first African–American president of U.S.

1950   **1990**   **2010**

KEY PEOPLE

Aristotle (384–322 BCE)
Aristotle was born in Stagira, Greece, the son of a physician. When he was 17 he went to study at the Academy in Athens, which was then the greatest seat of learning in the world, before founding his own school, the Lyceum. Aristotle's writings spanned all branches of human knowledge, from zoology to politics and made a lasting impact on the thoughts and scientific discoveries of later civilizations. In *A History of Animals* and *On the Generation of Animals,* he described the characteristics of different animal species and attempted to explain their behavior.

Ludwig Boltzmann (1844–1906)
Boltzmann was a Vienna-born physicist who was a firm believer in the existence of atoms and molecules at a time when many others did not. His most important work included an equation for calculating the speed of molecules in a gas.

Robert Boyle (1627–1691)
Born in County Waterford, Ireland, Boyle was one of the founders of modern chemistry. At Oxford University he and Robert Hooke (1635–1703) devised a vacuum chamber, and they used this for many experiments on gas behavior. Boyle understood that gases were made up of tiny particles, and he was the first to define the modern idea of a chemical element.

Henry Cavendish (1731–1810)
Cavendish was born in France, to English parents. He studied at Cambridge University, though he didn't graduate. He was very shy and extremely modest about his scientific revelations, many of which were only discovered long after his death. By combining metals with strong acids, Cavendish made hydrogen gas, which he isolated and studied. Although others had already isolated hydrogen, Cavendish recognized that it was an element, which he called "inflammable air." His electrical experiments led him to discover the concept of electric potential, the relationship between electric potential and current, now called Ohm's Law, and much more.

Marie Curie (1867–1934)
Curie was born Maria Sklodowska in Warsaw, Poland. She became a student at the Sorbonne, Paris, in 1891, where she met the physicist Pierre Curie, whom she married in 1895. Together they discovered the elements polonium and radium in 1898 and were awarded the Nobel Prize for physics five years later. They also pioneered the study of the natural flow of energy called radiation. Marie's belief that radiation comes from within atoms themselves was the start of the new science of nuclear physics. In 1911 she was awarded the Nobel Prize for chemistry.

John Dalton (1766–1844)
English chemist John Dalton was born in Cumberland, then moved to Manchester where he taught math. He researched meteorology and color-blindness (or Daltonism), from which he suffered. But he is best known for his work with gases and liquids. Dalton put forward his atomic theory in 1803, stating that chemical elements are made up of indivisible atoms that combine to form compounds. He also devised a set of symbols to represent the known elements.

Antoine Lavoisier (1743–1794)
A native of Paris, France, Lavoisier was one of the greatest chemists of the 18th century. He is particularly well known for his work with oxygen, which he both recognized and named. Lavoisier also understood the crucial importance of this element for combustion and for animal and plant respiration. He wrote the first version of the law of conservation of matter and disproved phlogiston theory.

James Clerk Maxwell (1831–1879)

Scottish physicist Maxwell was born in Edinburgh and attended the university in that city before moving first to Cambridge University then to Aberdeen University, where he was a professor at the very young age of 25. His most productive period was while he was at King's College, London, between 1860 and 1865. Then, he would often attend lectures at the Royal Institution, where he came into regular contact with the famous British scientist Michael Faraday. It was during this period that Maxwell predicted the existence of electromagnetic radiation and concluded that light is just part of the spectrum of electromagnetic radiation.

Dmitri Mendeleyev (1834–1907)

Dmitri Ivanovich Mendeleyev was born, the youngest of 14 children, in the Russian town of Tobolsk. His mother ran the local glass factory, but in 1847, after the factory burned down, she took Dmitri to St. Petersburg. By 1866 Mendeleyev was professor of chemistry at the city's university. Three years later he announced his discovery of the Periodic Table of the elements, which was to make him the most famous Russian chemist of his time. The element mendelevium (number 101) was named for him.

Joseph Priestley (1733–1804)

Priestly was born in England and even as a young boy was interested in experiments. When he was 11 he tried to work out how long a spider would live in a bottle if deprived of air. When he was older he established a laboratory and became friends with the American scientist Benjamin Franklin. In 1767 he invented carbonated water, and seven years later he jointly (with the Swedish chemist Carl Scheele, 1742–1786) discovered oxygen, which he called "dephlogisticated air." He was persecuted for supporting the French Revolution (1789) and was forced to flee to Pennsylvania with his family in 1794.

Ernest Rutherford (1871–1937)

Rutherford was born in Brightwater, New Zealand, but won a scholarship to Cambridge University in 1895 before becoming a professor of physics at McGill University, Canada. There he studied radiation emissions and, with English radiochemist Frederick Soddy (1877–1956), formulated the laws of radioactive decay in 1905. He was awarded the Nobel Prize for chemistry in 1908. Rutherford published his nuclear model of the atom in 1911, and eight years later became director of the renowned Cavendish laboratory at Cambridge. He bombarded nitrogen atoms with alpha particles, changing them into oxygen. In 1920 he predicted the existence of a subatomic particle called the neutron.

Thales of Miletus (625–546 BCE)

The philosopher Thales was the first of the ancient Greeks to attempt to explain natural phenomena without reference to mythology. He advanced people's understanding of geometry, was the first to study electricity, and tried to work out the nature of matter.

J. J. Thomson (1856–1940)

Joseph John Thomson was born near Manchester, England. He trained as a railroad engineer, before attending Cambridge University. Thomson deflected cathode rays with electric and magnetic fields, and he showed that they travel more slowly than light waves. He also discovered that cathode rays consisted of minuscule negatively charged particles, which he called "corpuscles." Although another scientist (George Stoney, 1826–1911) had already predicted the existence of these particles and called them electrons, it was Thomson who provided the proof.

GLOSSARY

alchemy An early form of chemistry which aimed to turn ordinary metals into gold.

alpha particle Large radioactive particle identical to the nucleus of a helium atom.

apeiron Universal substance thought to form all matter by Anaximander.

atom The smallest particle of a chemical element.

base metal Metal such as lead that alchemists tried to turn into gold.

bond The force that holds atoms together in a molecule.

caloric theory An early theory that suggested heat was a substance that flowed like a liquid.

compound A chemical substance made by joining different elements.

chemistry The science of studying the composition, structure, and properties of substances, and the changes they undergo.

electrolysis A method of separating a compound into its elements using electricity.

electron A tiny, negatively charged particle that exists inside atoms.

element A chemical that cannot be separated into simpler substances using only chemical means.

kinetic theory The idea that substances behave as they do because of the moving molecules within them.

mass The amount of matter.

matter The substance from which things are made.

molecule A structure made by joining two or more atoms.

nanotechnology A method of building microscopic machines from atoms or molecules.

neutron An uncharged particle in the nucleus of an atom.

nucleus The central part of an atom.

organic chemistry The study and practical uses of carbon and its compounds.

particle accelerator Machine that makes particles move very fast before smashing them together to reveal their subatomic contents.

periodic table A way of arranging the chemical elements so that ones with similar properties are grouped in columns.

physics The science of studying matter and energy and the ways they interact.

proton A positively charged particle in the nucleus of an atom.

quantum A packet of energy. Two or more quantums are called quanta.

quantum theory The theory of the microscopic world inside atoms.

quark A basic particle from which larger particles such as protons and neutrons are made.

radioactivity The particles given off when unstable atoms decay (or change) into smaller, more stable atoms.

reaction A chemical change in which one set of elements and compounds (the reactants) turns into a different set of elements and compounds (the products).

relative atomic mass The mass of an atom compared to the mass of one-twelfth of a carbon atom. This gives hydrogen a value of 1 unit.

shell The orbit occupied by an electron as it circuits a nucleus.

subatomic particle Particles that together form an atom, such as electrons, protons, and neutrons.

thermodynamics The study of the transfer of energy, in the form of heat, during chemical reactions.

transmutation In alchemy, turning one material into another.

valency The number of chemical bonds that an atom can form with other atoms.

FOR MORE INFORMATION

BOOKS

Aloian, Molly. *Atoms and Molecules*. New York, NY: Crabtree, 2009.

Aloian, Molly. *Mixtures and Solutions.* New York, NY: Crabtree, 2009.

Ballard, Carol. *Mixtures and Solutions*. Chicago, IL: Raintree, 2008.

Basher, Simon. *The Periodic Table. Elements with Style!* New York, NY: Kingfisher, 2007.

Claybourne, Anna. *Unlocking the Secrets of Atoms and Molecules*. Vero Beach, FL: Rourke, 2008.

Gardner, Robert. *Chemistry Projects With a Laboratory You Can Build*. Berkeley Heights, NJ: Enslow, 2008.

Gore, Bryson. *Chemistry: The Story of Atoms and Elements*. Mankato, MN: Stargazer Books, 2009.

Green, Dan. *Chemistry: Getting a Big Reaction*. New York, NY: Kingfisher, 2010.

Lepora, Nathan. *Atoms and Molecules*. New York, NY: Marshall Cavendish, 2011.

Morgan, Sally. *From Greek Atoms to Quarks: Discovering Atoms*. Chicago, IL: Heinemann Library, 2011.

Saunders, Nigel. *Chemical Reactions*. New York, NY: Rosen, 2008.

Winston, Robert. *It's Elementary! Putting the Crackle into Chemistry*. New York, NY: Dorling Kindersley, 2010.

Yount, Lisa. *Antoine Lavoisier: Founder of Modern Chemistry*. Berkeley Heights, NJ: Enslow, 2008.

WEB SITES

Due to the changing nature of Internet links, Rosen Publishing has developed an online list of Web sites related to the subject of this book. This site is updated regularly. Please use this link to access this list:

http://www.rosenlinks.com/scipa/atom

INDEX